Understanding Authority For Effective Leadership

Understanding Authority For Effective Leadership

*by
Dr. Doyle "Buddy" Harrison*

HARRISON HOUSE
Tulsa, Oklahoma

Unless otherwise indicated, all Scripture quotations are taken from the *King James Version* of the Bible.

6th Printing
Over 40,000 in Print

Understanding Authority
For Effective Leadership
ISBN 0-89274-379-4
(previously ISBN 0-89274-218-6)
Copyright © 1982 by Buddy Harrison
P. O. Box 35443
Tulsa, Oklahoma 74153

Published by Harrison House, Inc.
P. O. Box 35035
Tulsa, Oklahoma 74153

Printed in the United States of America. All rights reserved under International Copyright Law. Contents and/or cover may not be reproduced in whole or in part in any form without the express written consent of the Publisher.

Contents

Foreward
Acknowledgment
Introduction

1	Restoration of Authority	15
2	God—The Supreme Authority	27
3	Levels of Authority Under God	37
4	Leadership	73
5	Submission or Obedience?	95
6	Ruling With Liberty	113

Foreword

In this excellent book, *Understanding Authority For Effective Leadership*, my son-in-law, Buddy Harrison, reveals the "secrets" of his success in the ministry.

Buddy went from being music youth director in his home church to holding several positions in my ministry. Then God promoted him to pastoring, evangelizing, and leadership roles in the Body of Christ. But it didn't come easily.

Through the years I have watched Buddy's struggles and have prayed for him. He forged ahead through the difficult years relentlessly, working, weeping, and seeking God. Under the direction and power of the Holy Spirit, Buddy's mind was renewed by the Word of God and his life was transformed.

The principles Buddy learned in his years of preparation for the ministry form a strong foundation for this book. Buddy points out, "It requires an understanding of the principles of authority in order to understand the elements of faith. If we misapply authority, we will miss the elements of faith."

I especially enjoyed Buddy's fresh insights into my favorite portion of Scripture on faith—Mark 11:23,24.

Buddy shows how God wants men and women to be free, even though mankind often seems to prefer slavery. He discusses principles of authority that apply between husbands and wives, and ministers and their flocks.

He points out that it is the responsibility of laymen "to analyze the quality of leadership that is before it and decide whether to accept or reject that leadership." And he counsels leaders to keep their motives pure.

Buddy's excellent counsel will do much to dispel, Biblically, the erroneous "discipleship" teaching that has come along in recent years, leading people off into needless bondage.

This is a book to be studied carefully in an age when authority is being misused and abused.

Kenneth E. Hagin

Acknowledgment

When the Lord spoke to my heart concerning the sovereignty of God, I started on a search for truth. I found some on my own, but I received a great deal more from the teaching of Ralph Mahoney. As I absorbed and digested the words he spoke, they became real to me, and God had more revelation to go with it. I will be eternally grateful to Ralph Mahoney for the truth he brought to my life through his tapes.

The basics of this book were derived from his tapes, coupled with knowledge which I previously possessed, and more revelation and insight from God which has brought us to this point. Thank God, this is not the end. There is more to come.

Introduction

Whenever you talk about miracles, you touch the area of the sovereignty of God. People automatically identify a miracle by referring to it as "a sovereign act of God." But one time the Spirit of God spoke to me, saying, "Have you ever noticed that the word *sovereign* is not in the New Testament?" I couldn't think of a scripture at that moment, so I began to study it out. To my surprise, I found it to be true: The word *sovereign* is not used in the New Testament — not even once.

Therefore I realized there needed to be qualifications on exactly what we mean when using certain terminology. When speaking about sovereignty, we must begin by examining the subject of authority; so when this began to stir inside me, the first thing I did was refer to a dictionary.

I found three meanings for the word *authority:*

•*power to influence.* For instance, a policeman has the power to influence. When he holds up his hand to oncoming traffic, he has authority over those drivers. He has the power to influence them to stop. If they fail to be influenced, then they will suffer the consequences.
•*persons in command.* A person who has authority is a person who has command or responsibility in a given situation.
•*grounds, or convincing force.* A synonym for *authority* is influence or power. The word *power* can be used in the same sense as *authority.* In translating the Bible, many times the word *power* is used meaning ability. Therefore, you must rightly divide the Word of God.

In researching the Old Testament, I discovered that the Hebrew only uses one word translated *authority,* which is used twice. The one scripture which applies in this case is Proverbs 29:2 which says, **When the righteous are in authority the people rejoice.** The word for authority in the Hebrew language means "to increase." This is quite enlightening when you think about the righteous having authority, or the ability to increase. After all, part of the blessing of God causes increase.

In researching the Greek, I found seven different words in defining *authority*. Four of them were nouns; three were verbs. First we will look at the meanings as nouns.

A noun stands for a person, place, or thing. The meanings of authority as a noun are:

- *lawful or liberty*. The word *authority* can also mean liberty, freedom, or that which is lawful.
- *upon order, or commandment*. When someone gives you a command to do a certain thing, it is because they have authority to give orders.
- *high place, or excellency*. God is high above, and we are seated with Him in heavenly places, or in places of authority.
- *power, might, or potentate*. When someone has power, he has authority.

A verb has to do with action. The three definitions of *authority* as a verb are:

- *power*, or the authority of God in force, in operation, in manifestation.
- *to exercise authority at home.*

• *self-working, or dominion.* The Scriptures teach that we have dominion. God has given us dominion on earth. When someone has dominion, it means he can act on his own.

It may seem as though many of the definitions are being repeated, but I want you to get a complete picture. There is more involved here than just one meaning; there are several types and levels of authority.

We need to understand the importance of authority. Without authority to do certain things, we can get into trouble. Without the understanding of how to utilize the authority we have, we can be hurt.

There are instances in the Bible where people have endeavored to exercise authority when they didn't have the right to. For example: in Acts 19:13-16 the seven sons of Sceva attempted to cast out an evil spirit **by (the name of) Jesus whom Paul preacheth.** Needless to say, they carried no authority. In fact, the evil spirit overcame all seven of them, tore off their clothes, and chased them down the street!

On the other hand, there is a perfect example of understanding authority in Matthew, chapter 8. In verse 8,9 a Roman centurion says to Jesus:

Lord, I am not worthy that thou shouldest come under my roof: but speak the word only, and my servant shall be healed.

For I am a man under authority, having soldiers under me: and I say to this man, Go, and he goeth; and to another, Come, and he cometh; and to my servant, Do this, and he doeth it.

Here is what the centurion was implying to Jesus: "You have authority. Therefore, if You speak the word only, my servant will be healed."

Jesus replied to the centurion in this way: **I have not found so great faith, no, not in Israel** (v. 9). What was so great about the centurion's faith? He understood the principles of authority.

It requires an understanding of the principles of authority in order to understand the elements of faith. If we misapply authority, we will miss the elements of faith. No person will ever receive God's best in the realm of faith until he understands these basic principles of authority, which brings us to the purpose of this book: to present these basic principles in a simple form as God has shared in His Word.

I pray that, as you read, you will open your heart and allow the Spirit of God to minister this truth to you—that you may have a greater understanding of the connection between the principles of authority and the elements of faith.

1
Restoration of Authority

Being born on the earth entitles you to certain rights and privileges, just like being born in the United States automatically makes you a legal citizen. You didn't have to sign any papers. You didn't have to do anything. Just the fact that you were born in this country makes you a citizen.

There is only one way to obtain authority on earth, and that is to be born here. You have been given a certain amount of authority as a result of your birth. Birth becomes your legal entry on this earth. It is necessary to be born on earth in order to have authority here.

God created man to fellowship and work with. When He created the earth, He gave Adam dominion to rule and reign. God and Adam walked and talked together in the Garden. They were close friends. They communed with one another. But as a result of taking heed to the words of the devil, Adam committed high treason. He sold to Satan that which was rightfully his.

Second Corinthians 4:4 declares Satan as the god of this world. How did Satan gain this authority? Adam gave it to him. Because God was just and fair, He would not come as a thief and take back what Satan had rightfully obtained from Adam. Instead, in order to restore man's authority, He made a plan which was upright and legal.

The only possible way to bring deliverance to man is to have legal rights in the earth, so it became necessary for Jesus to be born of a woman. Jesus became the incarnate God — a combination of God and man. Being born of a woman gave Jesus legal right to operate here. This introduced God's plan to purchase man.

Let's read the actual account of the conception of Jesus in Luke, chapter 1, beginning with verse 26:

And in the sixth month the angel Gabriel was sent from God unto a city of Galilee, named Nazareth, to a virgin espoused to a man whose

name was Joseph, of the house of David; and the virgin's name was Mary.

And the angel came in unto her, and said, Hail, thou that art highly favoured, the Lord is with thee: blessed art thou among women.

And when she saw him, she was troubled at his saying, and cast in her mind what manner of salutation this should be.

And the angel said unto her, Fear not, Mary: for thou hast found favour with God. And, behold, thou shalt conceive in thy womb, and bring forth a son, and shalt call his name JESUS. He shall be great, and shall be called the Son of the Highest: and the Lord God shall give unto him the throne of his father David: and he shall reign over the house of Jacob for ever; and of his kingdom there shall be no end.

Then said Mary unto the angel, How shall this be, seeing I know not a man?

That was a legitimate question; Mary had never been with a man. Yet this angel was giving her a message from God. You must fully realize the fact that this angel was speaking the Word of God to her. It was not the words of an angel; it was God's Word. The angel was just delivering it. The Word of God is spirit and life.

So Mary questioned the angel, saying, How shall this be, seeing I know not a man?

And the angel answered and said unto her, The Holy Ghost shall come upon thee, and the power of the Highest shall overshadow thee: therefore also that holy thing which shall be born of thee shall be called the Son of God.

And, behold, thy cousin Elisabeth, she hath also conceived a son in her old age: and this is the sixth month with her, who was called barren.

For with God nothing shall be impossible.

And Mary said, Behold the handmaid of the Lord; be it unto me according to thy word. And the angel departed from her.

People have accepted the virgin birth because it is in the Word of God. Yet they don't comprehend it. The mind cannot understand how a virgin could conceive a child when she had never known a man. Consequently, it has taken away from the virgin birth. However, if taken away from that, it will destroy the foundation for everything we believe.

There is a very real, simple answer in the Word of God that has been overlooked for years. God is a spirit, so anything He does, He does by means of the spirit. His words are spirit and life. Therefore when He speaks, His words create. Any word spoken by God will create, even when delivered by an angel.

Verse 37 says, **For with God nothing shall be impossible.** The *American Standard Version* says, **No word of God shall be void of power.** Therefore, the words God spoke to Mary through the angel contained the power necessary to create life within her. All that was needed at that point was Mary's approval, her willingness to receive those creative words of Almighty God. And Mary said, **Behold the handmaid of the Lord; be it unto me according to thy word.**

There is truth in the saying, "Where there is a will, there is a way." Many people never accomplish God's will in their lives because they have not willed to do so. Unless you purposely set your will to accomplish a particular thing, it will never be done. God set His will to purchase man's authority. James 1:18 says,

Of his own will begat he us with the word of truth. God didn't have to do it. He didn't have to send Jesus, but He willed to do it. **For God so loved the world, that he gave his only begotten Son** (John 3:16). He sent His Son, not to just a select few, but to the entire world — to all of us!

For years after I was saved I didn't understand what had actually happened, but I was glad that it did happen. I knew my salvation was real, but it sure helps when your head understands. Then I found out I needed to renew my mind to the Word of God. This is why many theologians have never figured out the Gospel: they can't understand it with their minds.

The Gospel is not a mental revelation; it is a spiritual revelation, given by the Spirit of God. The Word of God is powerful enough to make it alive inside you if you will allow it to. However, most people won't open themselves to the Word of God.

Restoration of Authority

Isaiah prophesied of that which was to come in the days ahead. In chapter 9, verses 6 and 7, he writes:

For unto us a child is born, unto us a son is given: and the government shall be upon his shoulder: and his name shall be called Wonderful, Counsellor, The mighty God, The everlasting Father, The Prince of Peace.

Of the increase of his government and peace there shall be no end, upon the throne of David, and upon his kingdom, to order it, and to establish it with judgment and with justice from henceforth even for ever. The zeal of the Lord of hosts will perform this.

Isaiah is speaking of Jesus. This was the beginning of our restoration. Satan had become god of this world. The birth of Jesus marked the beginning of restoration. Many people have never understood their authority; therefore, they have not entered into it.

Notice verse 6: **...and the government shall be upon his shoulder.** The word *government* got my attention. When you think of government, you think of the federal government, the state government, or your local government. Governments determine how things are to function. They have the final say as they rule and reign over their jurisdiction.

The Spirit of God prompted me to look up the word *government*, and I discovered that it came from a Hebrew word which leads to the word *empire*. When you think of the word *empire*, you think of large corporations or an individual like Howard Hughes, who built an empire through his wealth. His companies amassed a fortune. In other words, when we speak of *empire* or *government*, we think of power, ability, and money. An actual meaning of the word *government* is "to prevail, or to have power."

...and the government shall be upon his shoulder. Another phrase for government is "princely power." Jesus is the Prince of Peace. Notice verse 7: **Of the increase of his government and peace there shall be no end.**

Whether or not you have realized it, you are part of an empire. You are to carry on, function, and operate as such. For years, Christians have thought, "I'm just an old sinner, saved by grace. I hope I make it through the day." But, in reality, a Christian is one who has princely power, who has authority.

Jesus has always had authority in heaven. When He came to live on earth, His authority was obtained through His birth. When Jesus died and went to hell, He beat Satan. The Bible says, ...**he made a shew of them openly, triumphing over them in it** (Col. 2:15). Jesus obtained authority through the Resurrection. He rose triumphant, obtaining the keys of death, hell, and the grave. He achieved authority in three worlds: heaven, earth, and under the earth.

After His resurrection, Jesus delivered that authority unto us, the Body of Christ. We are not merely saved by grace; we have princely powers vested in us. We have authority because we are part of His government. Jesus set up a spiritual kingdom. Anything that begins in the spirit realm will manifest itself in the physical realm. The authority we have in the spirit realm will manifest in the physical as well.

When you pray, the government that is operating in the natural realm will have to conform to the Word of God. When you begin to speak, things begin to change. Though you may be bound physically, you are free in the spiritual realm. We have princely power — an ability with God.

Once Jesus obtained authority and gave it to us, the complete restoration had taken place. The entire plan of God had been accomplished. Jesus is seated in heaven, at the right hand of the Father. (Mark 16:19.) Do you sit down when there is a job to be done? No! That means Jesus has completed His part.

Now we must do our part. But how do we do it? Simply by speaking the Word, even as Mary did: **Be it unto me according to thy word.** This is the thing you must remind yourself of. You must go back and rest in the Word of God, even as Mary rested. You must say, "Be it done unto me even as Thou hast said."

Our authority has been restored. Now allow the things that God has spoken to your heart to become dominant and powerful in your life. Trust and rely on God. Take His Word, speak it, then rest in it, and God will have an open channel to work in you. He had an open channel with Mary in the same manner.

Who can be against you? What is there to stop you from doing what God has called you to do?

You say, "But I don't have the money to do it." That may be true, but you have the authority to change it. How do you change it? Even as Mary did: receive the Word of God and declare, "Be it done unto me even as Thou hast said. The Word of God declares that my God shall supply all my need according to His riches in glory by Christ Jesus."

Quit trying to figure it out. Just receive the Word. Then the Holy Ghost will overshadow it and begin to cause it to explode inside you. It will erupt with life abundant. The Word of God is not void of power; it is well able.

2
God—The Supreme Authority

Let every soul be subject unto the higher powers. For there is no power but of God: the powers that be are ordained of God.

Whosoever therefore resisteth the power, resisteth the ordinance of God: and they that resist shall receive to themselves damnation.

For rulers are not a terror to good works, but to the evil. Wilt thou then not be afraid of the power? do that which is good, and thou shalt have praise of the same:

For he is the minister of God to thee for good. But if thou do that which is evil, be afraid; for he beareth not the sword in vain: for he is the minister of God, a revenger to execute wrath upon him that doeth evil.

Wherefore ye must needs be subject, not only for wrath, but also for conscience sake. For this cause pay ye tribute also: for they are God's ministers, attending continually upon this very thing.

Render therefore to all their dues: tribute to whom tribute is due; custom to whom custom; fear to whom fear; honour to whom honour.

Owe no man any thing, but to love one another: for he that loveth another hath fulfilled the law.
Romans 13:1-8

Remember, we have established the fact that the words *power* and *authority* are interchangeable in many instances. Here Paul is saying, **Let every soul be subject** (or more literally, stand under), **the higher powers** (the higher authority). **For there is no power** (authority) **but of God, the powers** (authorities) **that be are ordained of God.**

If God ordains all authorities, then He must be supreme authority. God is the author of authority; therefore, when we speak of the Lord God, we are speaking of a sovereign God. *Sovereign* means highest, supreme, and absolute.

In looking up the word *sovereignty*, one thing you will find is that it carries all of the above-mentioned meanings. However, in addition to these, the definition includes "unqualified." Some people say God has a supreme authority that is unqualified.

This is where I cannot agree with some teachers about the sovereignty of

God—The Supreme Authority

God. God is a supreme being, but *His authority is qualified*. God has never done anything unqualified because He holds Himself in subjection to His own Word. He will not permit certain things simply because of His Word. We need to understand that God does not run this world in a hit-and-miss method. There are laws that God has given which are in operation at all times.

God is the highest authority, a supreme being, Who holds Himself by a self-imposed law that will not allow Him to do certain things. For example, God has the ability to lie. He has the authority because He *is* final and total authority. However, His Word says He cannot lie. (Titus 1:2.) Therefore, He has qualified His ability and would not allow Himself to lie. The reason for this is that He would violate some of His other laws.

We can recognize that He is sovereign in the sense that He is supreme and highest, but He is not unqualified. He placed Himself under qualifications. He will *always* work within the guidelines of His Word.

The Lord put this definition in my heart: *The sovereignty of God is the operation of the laws of God, be they known or unknown.* You may or may not know the laws of God. That which you know you will be responsible for. There will be those that you don't know.

Laws work. They are absolute and will work regardless of whether or not you believe in them. Laws will always work unless they are superseded by a higher law.

It doesn't matter whether you believe in the law of gravity; it is going to work for you when you come in contact with it. If you jump off the top of a building, you will soon discover that the law of gravity works. It will always work because it is a law, an absolute. However, the law of lift will supersede the law of gravity. That doesn't mean the law of gravity has been done away with. It has only been superseded by another law.

In Ephesians 1:20-23 Paul prayed for the Church, saying:

...Which he wrought in Christ, when he raised him from the dead, and set him at his own right

hand in the heavenly places, far above all principality, and power, and might, and dominion, and every name that is named, not only in this world, but also in that which is to come:

And hath put all things under his feet, and gave him to be the head over all things to the church, which is his body, the fulness of him that filleth all in all.

This scripture establishes God as the sovereign God, the supreme God, the highest authority there is, far above all others. Also, it makes reference to certain levels of authority: principalities, powers, might, and dominion.

We need to understand the different types and levels of authority. As we have already seen, God is the supreme and highest authority. The first chapter of Hebrews includes a series of scriptures that adds support to this truth:

God, who at sundry times and in divers manners spake in time past unto the fathers by the prophets, hath in these last days spoken unto us by his Son, whom he hath appointed heir of all things, by whom also he made the worlds;

Who being the brightness of his glory, and the express image of his person, and upholding all things by the word of his power, when he had by himself purged our sins, sat down on the right hand of the Majesty on high;

Being made so much better than the angels, as he hath by inheritance obtained a more excellent name than they.

For unto which of the angels said he at any time, Thou art my Son, this day have I begotten thee? And again, I will be to him a Father, and he shall be to me a Son?

And again, when he bringeth in the firstbegotten into the world, he saith, And let all the angels of God worship him.

And of the angels he saith, Who maketh his angels spirits, and his ministers a flame of fire.

But unto the Son he saith, Thy throne, O God, is for ever and ever; a sceptre of righteousness is the sceptre of thy kingdom.

Thou hast loved righteousness, and hated iniquity; therefore God, even thy God, hath anointed thee with the oil of gladness above thy fellows.

Hebrews 1:1-9

Some people have misinterpreted this last verse: **...God, even thy God, hath anointed thee with the oil of gladness above thy fellows.** They say this means that the gifts ministries — those ministries in the Body of Christ demonstrating the gifts of the Holy Spirit — hold a higher position than their fellow believers.

God has not given authority to any man to usurp authority over another. He has given certain responsibilities which carry with it authority, but that does not mean they can rule and reign over others. We are to rule and reign over demons and evil spirits. If you want to usurp authority over someone, go after the devil, not other men.

I am endeavoring to show you that Jesus is above men. We are the Body of Christ, and Jesus—the Head of the Church—is above the Body. When you understand this, you will understand that Jesus is above all other elements. Since we are in the Body, that means all other elements are under our feet as well, which only enhances our understanding of the different levels of authority involved.

In speaking of Jesus, Revelation 19:13 says, **And he was clothed with a vesture dipped in blood: and his name is called The Word of God.** Jesus *is* the Word of God. Verse 16 says, **And he hath on his** vesture and on his thigh a name written, **KING OF KINGS, AND LORD OF LORDS.** This indicates without doubt that He is supreme and sovereign authority.

Because we are heirs of God and joint-heirs with Jesus, we are in a plan of authority. We are to reign as a king. Jesus is the King of kings and the Lord of lords. We are to rule as lords. Don't take away from His position, and don't put yourself in a wrong position. Take your position with Him and honor Him as the Head.

Some people have tried to exalt themselves to an important position. Some try to make themselves above God, which is the very thing that Satan tried to do. In Isaiah 14:13, we read how Lucifer said, **...I will exalt my throne above the stars of God.**

If you study this situation, you will find that Satan, or Lucifer, was in a key position from the very beginning. However, he was unsatisfied; he wanted to be above God. He used the law of God, only in the wrong way, so he perverted it. He was confessing it with his mouth

God—The Supreme Authority

and believing it in his heart, according to Mark 11:23; but because he used it for evil, his plan went sour.

There is one thing I want you to understand about sovereignty. Many times people have used the excuse, "It was a sovereign act of God," when in reality it was actually the law of God in operation. You see, people can operate in the laws of God and not even know it. Laws can be operative without understanding. When you understand the operation of the laws of God, you can use them to your benefit.

What most sovereignty teaching comes down to is putting the blame for failure on God. People don't want the responsibility of their own failure. They don't want "the monkey on their back."

I hear too many people saying, "Things just don't go right for me. I don't understand why." The answer is simply because they have worked the laws in the wrong way, in a negative manner.

The Bible clearly teaches that you can have what you say. (Mark 11:23,24.) When you say, "It doesn't work for me," you are actually working that law in its negative form. You have what you say, only the results you are receiving are not positive. Too often an event or occurrence is blamed on the "sovereignty of God," when actually God has delegated the authority to the people involved.

There is one fact we can be sure of: God is not our problem!

3
Levels of Authority Under God

In dealing with the subject of authority, many questions arise. How do we recognize authority? How do we deal with it? How do we know when and how we are to submit to the various levels of authority that exist?

There is a pattern that runs throughout every level of life, both spiritual and physical. When there is a conflict between persons in authority, the only solution is for the people involved to look to a higher authority. This higher authority will resolve the situation. We are to move to a higher authority to settle any issue or conflict that we face in life, be it natural or spiritual.

To understand authority to its fullest degree, we must recognize and know the various levels of authority that exist.

The Higher Powers

It is God's command that **every soul be subject unto the higher powers** (Rom. 13:1). What are these "higher powers"? Basically, there are three. As we learned in Chapter 2, the first and highest power, or authority, is God. He is the supreme authority of all creation. The other two positions of authority in this higher realm are truth and the conscience of man. No person has the right to violate these three levels of authority.

Veracious Authority—Truth

One type of authority that has been bypassed for years is called veracious authority. *Veracious* means truth. There is an authority that accompanies truth. Certain things produce authority simply because they are true. Jesus said, **Ye shall know the truth, and the truth shall make you free** (John 8:32).

From the standpoint of mathematics, we can use as an example the simple formula: $2 + 2 = 4$. This is not arbitrary. No matter how hard you try, you cannot make five out of it because that would not be true. Truth carries authority. When something is true, authority automatically goes with it. The fact that it is true gives it authority.

Jesus said, **I am the way, the truth, and the life** (John 14:6). From the moment that you find truth, it will begin to set you free. But it really is more than just seeing the truth; you must *know* the truth. The truth alone will never set you free; it is *knowing* the truth that sets you free. Everyone has been set free. Jesus paid the price for all of humanity; but many don't know it because they have not been told.

When we say *truth*, what are we speaking of? The Scriptures contain truth. They contain the words of Jesus, and we must know the words of Jesus to be set free.

There are certain things that must be qualified when saying the Scriptures are truth. The prophets of old wrote when they were moved upon by the Holy Spirit. Remember, the Holy Spirit is referred to as the Spirit of Truth. Therefore, when the Holy Spirit moved upon them, they wrote the truth. The words Jesus spoke were words of life and words of truth. We can simply say that there is authority because the Scriptures contain truth.

When someone tells a lie against you, it really doesn't matter. When the truth comes out, authority will reign. When the truth is *known*, everything is exonerated; everything becomes clean and changed. Why? Because truth carries authority.

There are a few statements regarding truth that I want to set out. You need to meditate on these:

Nothing contrary to Scripture can be truth.

Nothing in addition to Scripture can be binding. Any lie the Devil presents to you cannot be binding. When he says you are sick, you can answer, "No, I'm not! I'm healed because the Word of God says so." Why? Because the Word of God is truth.

Every believer is responsible to God to search the Scriptures and find the truth. This point is especially important because so many people have wrongly tried to exercise authority over another individual. Some people have been indoctrinated over the years to swallow

Levels of Authority Under God

whatever is fed to them. It is the responsibility of every believer to search the Scriptures and learn the truth.

Paul made this clear in Galatians 1:9. He wrote, **As we said before, so say I now again, if any man preach any other gospel unto you than that ye have received, let him be accursed.** Even if the greatest angel appears before you, don't believe what he says unless it agrees with the Word of God, regardless of the signs that may accompany him.

It makes no difference who a person is or how long he has been in the ministry, if his preaching does not line up with the Word, don't accept it. Furthermore, if you fail to check out what he teaches to see if it follows the Word, you are the one who is wrong.

And the brethren immediately sent away Paul and Silas by night unto Berea: who coming thither went into the synagogue of the Jews.

These were more noble than those in Thessalonica, in that they received the word with all readiness of mind, and searched the scriptures daily, whether those things were so.

Therefore many of them believed; also of honourable women which were Greeks, and of men, not a few.

Acts 17:10-12

Paul and Silas were doing the preaching, yet the people who heard them were questioning what they heard. They received the Word with readiness of mind; or in other words, they received the Word with openness. Yet, even when they heard God's Word from the Apostle Paul — a man who had more revelation than anyone — they still checked him by the Scriptures. They **searched the scriptures daily, whether these things were so.**

Remember, you must qualify what is meant by truth. **Everything in the Bible is truly stated, but not everything in the Bible is true.** The Biblical account of Job is a classic example. In recounting the incident, Job made this statement: **The Lord gave and the Lord hath taken away; blessed be the name of the Lord** (Job 1:21). This statement was truly recorded — Job *did* say those words — however, it is not a true statement. God is not the stealer; He is the life-giver. It was Satan who stole from Job!

Levels of Authority Under God

There is truth in God's Word, but the wisdom of God is hidden and must be searched for. As Paul said in his first epistle to Timothy:

Study to shew thyself approved unto God, a workman that needeth not to be ashamed, rightly dividing the word of truth.

2 Timothy 2:15

We need to show ourselves approved unto God by rightly dividing the Word of God. It is our responsibility, when we hear the Word ministered, to check it out.

Only when you prove the Word in your own heart will you be established and not tossed about with every wind of doctrine. (Eph. 4:14.) Become solid, concrete, and established in what you believe.

Authority of the Conscience

Let every soul be subject unto the higher powers...

Wherefore ye must needs be subject, not only for wrath, but also for conscience sake.

Romans 13:1,5

What is meant by the word *conscience*? When the Bible uses the term *conscience*, it is referring to the heart. *Conscience* can be broken down into two words: *co-* and *science. Co-* means two and *science* means knowledge.

Man is a product of two kinds of knowledge: a knowledge which comes from above and a knowledge that comes from within. This knowledge from within man is a product of his five physical senses. We receive spiritually in our hearts and mentally in our minds. Authority to act comes according to these two kinds of knowledge.

This by no means is the only application for the word *conscience* It is not necessarily a scholarly approach, but a basic concept to understand why things are the way they are.

Many times people become frustrated because they are receiving an input of information from both areas — spiritual and mental. Very often these two kinds of information conflict. This brings them to a point of confusion. Until they receive more knowledge, they will remain at that point of confusion.

Jesus said, **Ye shall know the truth, and the truth shall make you free** (John

Levels of Authority Under God

8:32). Only by obtaining the truth can you reach a place of freedom and be rid of that confusion and bondage.

Some people say that they don't know right from wrong, but that is not true. Any person whose mind is functioning normally can know right from wrong. Right and wrong can be measured by how you want to be treated by other people. For example, if someone steals your car, you know that person has done wrong. Why? Because the car belongs to you, and that person has no right to take it. If you know when wrong is done to you, then you know right from wrong. When something wrong is wrong to you, then it is wrong for you to do it to others.

When people say they can't tell right from wrong, they are either kidding themselves or lying. God's commandments were established to distinguish right from wrong. When a certain act brings damaging effects, it is wrong.

When speaking of *conscience*, or co-knowledge, we mean knowledge of the heart and knowledge of the head. Much of it depends upon our attitude towards situations.

For as many as have sinned without the law shall also perish without the law; and as many as have sinned in the law shall be judged by the law;

(For not the hearers of the law are just before God, but the doers of the law shall be justified. For when the Gentiles, which have not the law, do by nature the things contained in the law, these, having not the law, are a law unto themselves: which shew the work of the law written in their hearts, their conscience also bearing witness, and their thoughts the mean while accusing or else excusing one another;)

In the day when God shall judge the secrets of men by Jesus Christ according to my gospel.
> Romans 2:12-16

This scripture explains how people that have never heard the Gospel are going to be judged. Verse 15 says, **...which shew the work of the law written in their hearts, their conscience also bearing witness.** They are going to know by their conscience and will be judged according to their conscience. This means that the conscience must carry authority.

You may ask, "How can the person who has never heard the Gospel accept Jesus as Lord and Savior?"

They have some knowledge of God because the very firmaments declare the glory of God. They have to recognize the existence of a Supreme Authority through the firmaments of the heavens, though they may not know His name. Paul addressed the people at Athens this way: **For as I passed by, and beheld your devotions, I found an altar with this inscription, TO THE UNKNOWN GOD. Whom therefore ye ignorantly worship, him declare I unto you** (Acts 17:23). Though these people had never heard the Glad Tidings — the Good News — they worshipped an unknown God. Paul used this unknown God to make known unto them Jesus.

The fact that you have a conscience will qualify you to be either accused or excused.

For the kingdom of God is not meat and drink; but righteousness, and peace, and joy in the Holy Ghost.

For he that in these things serveth Christ is acceptable to God, and approved of men.

Let us therefore follow after the things which make for peace, and things wherewith one may edify another.

For meat destroy not the work of God. All things indeed are pure; but it is evil for that man who eateth with offence.

It is good neither to eat flesh nor to drink wine, nor any thing whereby thy brother stumbleth, or is offended, or is made weak.

Hast thou faith? have it to thyself before God. Happy is he that condemneth not himself in that thing which he alloweth.

And he that doubteth is damned if he eat, because he eateth not of faith: for whatsoever is not of faith is sin.

Romans 14:17-23

Notice verse 22: **Happy is he that condemneth not himself in that thing which he alloweth.** How did he allow it? He allowed it in his conscience; his heart and his head agreed.

The knowledge you receive from your heart and from your head forms your conscience. The knowledge of the Word of God supersedes natural knowledge; therefore, you must act on the Word. If you fail to, your heart will condemn you. When your heart knows to do the Word of God, but you rebel, your heart will condemn you.

Some people argue and debate over which day we are to worship. Most people say Sunday, but some say Saturday. You can debate all day, but you

Levels of Authority Under God

have been made free to choose. If you study the Bible, you will find that actually we are supposed to worship seven days a week.

If a man believes he is supposed to worship on Saturday, but instead worships on Sunday, he will be condemning his own heart, violating the authority that is within him. God has much to say concerning the authority of the conscience.

Many people try to dictate to others what they can or cannot do, even when it is not their place to do so. Each individual is responsible to prove the Word of God in his own heart. Declare and do that which you know to do. It is not your place to judge others. Your conscience will be the thing that will govern the authority in which you operate. If you violate that authority, then it is your responsibility to pay the penalty.

Lower Levels of Authority

Within the confines of planet earth, there are several levels of authority: delegated authority, stipulated authority, functional authority, and authority in custom.

Delegated Authority

Obey them that have the rule over you and submit yourselves: for they watch for your souls, as they that must give account, that they may do it with joy, and not with grief: for that is unprofitable for you.

Hebrews 13:17

This scripture is establishing delegated authority. The police operate within the realm of delegated authority. God has given them the privilege and responsibility of ruling over us according to the laws of the land. Their authority has been delegated unto them. However, the instruction that we are to obey those who have the rule over us can apply to the spiritual realm as well as the natural.

We, as believers, have an authority that has been delegated to us by God, and there is a responsibility that comes with acting on authority.

The Lord has delegated certain responsibilities to the fivefold ministry gifts — apostle, prophet, evangelist, pastor, and teacher. Some have tried to present their authority in such a fashion that you have to do what they say, when they say, and how they say. However, God has not delegated to any man that type of authority.

The word *rule* in the Greek language simply means "to give shepherdlike leadership." To rule does not mean to lord it over someone, but to lead like a shepherd would. A shepherd cares. He loves. He guides. He would even lay down his life for the flock.

The first person we think of when referring to shepherdlike leadership is Jesus for He is the Great Shepherd. He is the perfect example of a leader, and He never ruled or lorded over anyone.

Authority and responsibility — these two words go hand in hand. **Authority proceeds only out of responsibility.** They are on an equal level. If you have been given the authority, it means you have the responsibility. If you have the responsibility, you should have the authority. It would be unjust for someone to give you the responsibility for a job and not give you the authority to act on it. God would never do that because the Bible says God

Understanding Authority For Effective Leadership

is just. If He gives you the responsibility for a particular job, He will give you the authority as well.

Authority never exceeds your responsibility. When your responsibility ends, your authority ends. Many times people have made mistakes by trying to take the authority for things they are not responsible for. They only end up in trouble.

Let me give you an illustration. Do you spank your neighbor's children? Your answer is probably, "No." Why not? Because that is not your responsibility. And if it is not your responsibility, then you have no authority in that area.

You may ask, "But what about teachers who spank children in school?"

Teachers have been given the responsibility to teach, to train, and to care for their students. They actually become mother and father to those children during the day. They have become your agents and are taking your place; therefore, they have the authority. You gave them that authority when you gave them the responsibility to teach and train the children.

Levels of Authority Under God

It would be pointless to give teachers the responsibility of teaching, training, and caring for your children without giving them the authority to correct them. With responsibility comes authority.

Now then we are ambassadors for Christ, as though God did beseech you by us: we pray you in Christ's stead, be ye reconciled to God.
2 Corinthians 5:20

The authority which God has given us can be likened to the authority given to an ambassador. The authority given to an ambassador is delegated to him, and he can only act to the limits of that authority.

When I was working for Brother Kenneth Hagin, I managed the office while he was on the road. One of the responsibilities I had was answering his mail. When the mail came in, I would call him on the phone and he would tell me what to write in response. Then he would say, "Sign my name to it." He gave me the authority to sign his name. The responsibility of answering the mail was mine, and along with it came the authority. I was his ambassador, his agent, acting on his behalf.

The same principle applies in dealing with insurance companies and their agents. The insurance agent is not the company; he is merely its representative. The agent acts on behalf of the company in its best interest. He has been delegated the authority to write policies, to pay claims, and to handle the routine business involved.

God has delegated authority to the Body of Christ. We are His ambassadors. What is the extent of our authority? We are to reconcile the world to God, to give them the Good News in Christ's stead. If Jesus was on earth today, He would still be preaching, teaching, and laying hands on the sick. But Jesus is not here; therefore, we have become His agents, His ambassadors. He has delegated authority to the Church. God is not going to ask you to cast out demons without giving you the authority to do so. There is nothing to be afraid of — the authority has been delegated to you.

However, if you don't act on the responsibility given to you, you will never exercise the authority. The authority will

Levels of Authority Under God

be there, but it will never be utilized. It is necessary to understand who you are acting for. You are not acting in *your* name, but in the name of Jesus. It is His name which carries the authority.

Stipulated Authority

Whenever you are acting on the authority that has been delegated to another person, you must qualify that authority and specify exactly what you are responsible for. This is stipulated authority.

In stipulated authority, both in the natural realm and in the spiritual realm, you enter into a legal contract.

And Jacob loved Rachel; and said, (to her father), I will serve thee seven years for Rachel thy younger daughter.

And Laban said, It is better that I give her to thee, than that I should give her to another man: abide with me.

Genesis 29:18,19

Jacob entered into an agreement — a contract, a covenant — with Laban, Rachel's father. However, it was a stipulative agreement; there was a time limit put on their agreement.

And Jacob served seven years for Rachel; and they seemed unto him but a few days, for the love he had to her.

And Jacob said unto Laban, Give me my wife, for my days are fulfilled that I may go in unto her.

Genesis 29:20,21

Jacob made a stipulative agreement with Laban to work for seven years to win Rachel. At the end of that period of time, he came to Laban and proclaimed the fulfillment of the contract. He had fulfilled the stipulations of their agreement.

Whenever you have responsibilities that are stipulated, there are authorities that go with it. The authority is limited to the responsibilities. It is difficult to understand the different laws that are involved if you don't study and apply yourself. For example, unless you apply yourself, you will never understand the laws that govern flying. You must study to understand because there are many different laws in operation at all times. The law of lift and the law of gravity are opposites, as is the law of thrust and the law of drag. Before you can learn to fly,

Levels of Authority Under God

you must first comprehend the laws that are in operation.

That is where many believers get into trouble with spiritual matters. They don't take the time to study and comprehend the laws of God. They use opposing laws, then can't understand why it doesn't work for them.

When two different laws come into contact with one another, they begin to conflict. Most people don't know how to handle it. They are unable to put the proper laws into operation to get the desired result. That is why you must take the time to study and to show yourself approved unto God. (2 Tim. 2:15.) Examine the laws of God. Discover how they operate. Know which laws complement each other, and which laws are reciprocals (opposites).

Authority in Custom

And Laban gathered together all the men of the place, and made a feast.

And it came to pass in the evening, that he took Leah his daughter, and brought her to him (Jacob); and he went in unto her.

> And Laban gave unto his daughter Leah Zilpah his maid for an handmaid.
>
> And it came to pass, that in the morning, behold, it was Leah: and he said to Laban, What is this thou hast done unto me? did not I serve with thee for Rachel? wherefore then hast thou beguiled me?
>
> And Laban said, It must not be so done in our country, to give the younger before the firstborn.
>
> Fulfil her week, and we will give thee this also for the service which thou shalt serve with me yet seven other years.
>
> **Genesis 29:22-27**

Jacob had a stipulative agreement with Laban; however, another law superseded. There was an additional authority involved: custom.

There is a certain aspect of custom which can be either good or bad, depending upon how it is used. In this situation Laban made it work to his advantage. He utilized a law to work his own way. It may not have been right or fair, but it was a law.

In the New Testament, Paul deals with the subject of custom. **But if any man seem to be contentious, we have no such custom, neither the churches of God**

(1 Cor. 11:16). Paul is proving a point by saying there is no such custom; therefore, we see authority in custom. When there is a custom, it carries authority and it must be observed.

For example, if you go into a church where the congregation does not lift their hands and praise God, you will feel the influence of their authority when you lift your hands. The authority in their custom will affect your behavior. You may want to praise God, but the custom is ruling. Tradition carries authority.

Then came to Jesus scribes and Pharisees, which were of Jerusalem, saying,

Why do thy disciples transgress the tradition of the elders? for they wash not their hands when they eat bread.

But he answered and said unto them, Why do ye also transgress the commandment of God by your tradition?

For God commanded, saying, Honour thy father and mother: and, He that curseth father or mother, let him die the death.

But ye say, Whosoever shall say to his father or his mother, It is a gift, by whatsoever thou mightest be profited by me;

And honor not his father or his mother, he shall be free. Thus have ye made the commandment of God of none effect by your tradition.

Ye hypocrites, well did Esaias prophesy of you, saying,

This people draweth nigh unto me with their mouth, and honoureth me with their lips; but their heart is far from me.

But in vain they do worship me, teaching for doctrines the commandments of men.
Matthew 15:1-9

It is acceptable to have custom. There is a custom in our church that we clap our hands when we receive the offering, which is suitable as long as it lines up with the Word. Where people make their mistake is in trying to put custom or tradition above the Scriptures.

Functional Authority

There is authority in the way you function. More clearly, you have authority according to your abilities, be it by birth, training, or impartation. Some people just naturally have abilities by birth. Some are born with an ear for music. Musician Doyle Tucker is one of these people. Music with him is a natural thing, though

Levels of Authority Under God

he has added to it through training. When Doyle sits at the piano, there is authority that comes through his music.

Mathematics is an area that I have always been good in. I received it from my dad. Figuring percentages and adding figures is inherent with me. Yet I have an authority in other areas that I received by impartation. For example, when God called me to pastor, He said, "Go back to Tulsa. Start a family church, a charismatic teaching center, and reach the world." He told me to pastor supernaturally. I received the ability to pastor through impartation.

There is authority through impartation by the Spirit of God. For example, Smith Wigglesworth was a great man of God who received from God through impartation. He was middle-aged when he answered the call of God on his life. He was an uneducated man, who could neither read nor write, but God imparted to him the ability to read one book, the Bible.

Through the gift imparted to him by God, Wigglesworth became an authority concerning God's Word. As a result of his ministry, three men were raised from the dead and people were healed throughout the world. Wigglesworth functioned in an authority that few men understood, but was definitely of God.

There is an account of an incident in the ministry of Smith Wigglesworth that occurred while he was holding a three-day crusade. He had instructed the audience, "If I have ministered to you before, don't get in the line again." The healing power of God was at work within them, so there was no need to be prayed for again.

The second night a man on crutches decided he would be prayed for again, so he started up the stair to the platform. When that man came forward to have hands laid on him, Brother Wigglesworth said, "Didn't I minister to you last night?"

The man answered, "Yes, but I didn't get healed."

"Didn't get healed? Didn't get healed? Yes, you did! You just don't have sense enough to know it!" Wigglesworth turned him around and kicked him in the seat

Levels of Authority Under God

of the pants and off the platform. He knew the authority that had been imparted to him, and he operated in that authority.

One person in a church received the ability to play the piano through impartation. Though she had never played before and had no training, God suddenly gave her a gift. It was imparted to her by God.

Proverbs 18:16 says it this way: **A man's gift maketh room for him, and bringeth him before great men.** If you have a gift from God, whether it comes at birth, by training, or by impartation, that gift will make room for you. If you have ability in that area, it will show up.

Some people have diligently trained and developed abilitites in a particular area, so they can function with authority. Because they train and cultivate their abilities, authority is produced in their lives.

For example, suppose there is a traffic accident in which a woman is injured. Observing the accident are three men: a policeman, a mechanic, and a doctor.

Who will render medical aid and assistance to the woman? Will it be the mechanic? No. The policeman? No. It will be the doctor. Because he has training and ability in that area, he carries the authority.

The mechanic will be used according to his training. He has the authority to get the car in working condition. The doctor does not.

Because of the authority which the policeman carries, he will be used in still another area: to direct traffic and see to the official details of the accident. He will act on the authority he carries.

When a person functions in a particular realm of authority — whether by birth, by training, or by impartation — it would be foolish for someone else to try to function in that position without the authority. Why? Because he has no authority.

Once you know your position within the Body of Christ and understand what you are called to do, there is no reason to think about doing other things. As you train and develop in each area, you will

Levels of Authority Under God

be able to move on to higher things. Many people have never bothered to train themselves, so they are unequipped when the time comes to function.

For a time when I worked for Brother Kenneth Hagin, I read one book each day on business management or some facet of the areas we were involved in. When we began to produce cassette tapes, I began to study about cassettes. I could tell you the seventeen most critical points in a cassette. Because of the knowledge I obtained, it was possible for me to function with authority.

The same principles apply with regard to the home. We are to function within our abilities as husband, wife, parent, or child. Most husbands and wives miss it by trying to do things they are not equipped or qualified to do. For instance, the one in charge of paying bills should be the one who has the training and ability to do so. It does not necessarily have to be the man. If he is not smart enough, it would be foolish for him to do it. If some men didn't have a good wife to handle the finances, they would have failed a long time ago.

If the husband has abilities in that area, and he takes the responsibility, then he carries the authority that goes with it.

The important thing is to function within the abilities you have. My wife and I have an understanding in this area. I make the decisions as to which bills we pay and when; she writes the checks.

Wives, submit yourselves unto your own husbands, as unto the Lord (Eph. 5:22). The key to this verse is: **as unto the Lord.** How are you to submit to the Lord? In love. The same thing holds true for wives. All of this is done in love, in order that the husband and wife be a blessing to one another. They are to compliment one another: where one is weak, the other is strong.

Don't allow your marriage to become frustrated by trying to exercise authority when you haven't taken the responsibility. If you are going to take the authority, then be willing to take the responsibility that goes with it. As a husband, if you want to function as the head of your household, you must take on the responsibility—spirit, soul, and body.

Levels of Authority Under God

Ephesians 5:21 says, **Submitting yourselves one to another in the fear of God.** It is easy to submit yourselves one to another in the fear of the Lord when you are full of the presence and power of God. If you try to submit in a legalistic manner, you are going to moan and groan all the way. God never intended for that to be the case.

Many people try to exercise the wrong kind of authority in the wrong situation. Many times it is over someone else's will. In John 8:31 Jesus said, **If ye continue in my word, then are ye my disciples indeed.** The key words are: **continue in my word.** It did not say that to become a disciple you are to continue in the word of your pastor. Jesus said, "Continue in My Word."

You may ask, "Aren't we supposed to listen to the pastor?" Only if he is giving you the Word of God.

And Paul, earnestly beholding the council, said, Men and brethren, I have lived in all good conscience before God until this day.

And the high priest Ananias commanded them that stood by him to smite him on the mouth.

Then said Paul unto him, God shall smite thee, thou whited wall....
Acts 23:1-3

The chief apostle didn't turn the other cheek. There are three elements involved: the high priest, the chief apostle, and the Word of God. What did Paul become upset over? He continues in verse 3: **...for sittest thou to judge me after the law, and commandest me to be smitten contrary to the law?**

What was he arguing about? The law of God. He was struck on the head and he didn't appreciate it. It was contrary to the law of God. What authority was he appealing to? The authority of the Word, a higher authority.

And they that stood by said, Revilest thou God's high priest?

Then said Paul, I wist not, brethren, that he was the high priest: for it is written, Thou shalt not speak evil of the ruler of thy people.
Acts 23:4,5

Does this mean that Paul gave in? Yes, but not to the high priest. He gave in to the Word of God. He did not give in to a man, but to God's high priest. The Word of God had the higher authority.

Levels of Authority Under God

> Then came to him the mother of Zebedee's children with her sons, worshipping him, and desiring a certain thing of him.
>
> And he said unto her, What wilt thou? She saith unto him, Grant that these my two sons may sit, the one on thy right hand, and the other on the left, in thy kingdom.
>
> But Jesus answered and said, Ye know not what ye ask. Are ye able to drink of the cup that I shall drink of, and to be baptized with the baptism that I am baptized with? They say unto him, We are able.
>
> And he saith unto them, Ye shall drink indeed of my cup, and be baptized with the baptism that I am baptized with: but to sit on my right hand, and on my left, is not mine to give, but it shall be given to them for whom it is prepared of my Father.
>
> And when the ten heard it, they were moved with indignation against the two brethren.
>
> Matthew 20:20-24

The audacity of James and John to try to elevate themselves above the others! That is what people try to do. Satan tried it as the archangel Lucifer in heaven, and you know what happened to him!

Functional authority is serving people. That is one of the rules of the Kingdom.

Ephesians 2:19,20 makes this statement: **Now therefore ye are no more strangers and foreigners, but fellowcitizens with the saints, and of the household of God; and are built upon the foundation of the apostles and prophets, Jesus Christ himself being the chief corner stone.**

When you truly examine the family of God, you will find that those who are called to be apostles, prophets, evangelists, pastors, and teachers are at the bottom upholding it, not on the top ruling down. They are serving the Body of Christ.

According to 1 Peter 5:2, the responsibility of the fivefold ministry is this:

Feed the flock of God which is among you, taking the oversight thereof, not by constraint, but willingly; not for filthy lucre, but of a ready mind.

Neither as being lords over God's heritage, but being ensamples to the flock.

God does not intend for the ministry to be lord over you, but rather to be examples to you, to serve you and minister to you with the Word of God.

Levels of Authority Under God

In 2 Corinthians 1:24 the Apostle Paul wrote, **Not for that we have dominion over your faith....** Some people mistakenly try to exercise authority over the faith of others. That is not the responsibility of the ministry. The ministry is responsible only to prepare and deliver God's Word to the Body of Christ. Once that is done, it becomes your responsibility to receive that Word and act on it.

4
Leadership

Spiritual leadership is an awesome thing, carrying with it both authority and responsibility within the Body of Christ. If not handled properly, it can bring confusion to the work of God in the earth. But there is a responsibility within the Body of Christ to analyze the quality of leadership that is before it and decide whether to accept or reject that leadership.

The prophets prophesy falsely, and the priests bear rule by their means; and my people love to have it so: and what will ye do in the end thereof?

Jeremiah 5:31

There are times when leaders will take advantage of their position and utilize the authority given them in the wrong way. Not only is this the fault of the leaders, it is also the fault of those being led. By continuing to accept such leadership, they are condoning that wrongdoing. There is a responsibility on the part of every member in the Body of Christ to judge whether that which is coming from their leaders is of God.

Many pastors have destroyed my vineyard, they have trodden my portion under foot, they have made my pleasant portion a desolate wilderness.

They have made it desolate, and being desolate it mourneth unto me; the whole land is made desolate, because no man layeth it to heart.

Jeremiah 12:10,11

Many times people rise and fall with their leadership. Whatever the leadership does will reflect on those under them. For that reason, you must closely examine your leadership—who they are, what they are doing, and how they are doing it. A leader who is operating in fear will be afraid to let you know what he is doing, while one who is operating in faith and love will have no fear.

And it shall be, as with the people, so with the priest; as with the servant, so with his master; as with the maid, so with her mistress; as with the buyer, so with the seller; as with the lender, so with the borrower; as with the taker of usury, so with the giver of usury to him.

Isaiah 24:2

Leadership

The main point here is that everyone is responsible. There are leaders and there are followers. The blame for error cannot always be placed totally on the leadership. If the leaders are involved in error and the followers are aware of it, then it is the responsibility of those followers to do something about it. As long as they continue to follow, then they must accept a share of the blame.

Some horrible atrocities have occurred, such as the Jim Jones incident in Guyana, South America, in which several hundred people died at his command. We think how terrible Jim Jones must have been to lead hundreds of people to their deaths; but he would not have been able to lead them if they had not followed!

Followers have the responsibility to follow that which is correct.

God requires diligence of His people. In 2 Timothy 2:15 the Apostle Paul wrote, **Study to shew thyself approved unto God, a workman that needeth not to be ashamed, rightly dividing the word of truth.** Don't just accept anything and everything that comes your way. Look at your spiritual leaders. Examine the words they speak and the deeds of their lives. You are not to judge their hearts, but you can listen to them and determine if the words they speak line up with God's Word.

There is responsibility in leadership. In 2 Timothy 2:6 Paul said, **The husbandman that laboureth must be first partaker of the fruits.** In other words, the person who sits in a place of leadership must be a partaker of that which he says. It is not right to say, "Do as I say, but not as I do." If it isn't good enough for the leader to do, it isn't good enough for the follower.

The Lord told me some time ago that as a pastor I was to be an example to my flock. He said, "Any time a project comes up needing money, you give the first ten percent, regardless of the amount." Shortly after that, we held a missionary conference in which $45,000 was needed for the outreach—and ten percent of $45,000 is quite a sum of money. I decided to round off the figure to an even $5,000. At the time I needed $5,000 just for myself, much less giving it in sixty days

Leadership

as an offering to Mexico. It was a big step, but my faith was in God's Word.

I stood up and boldly said, "I will give the first $5,000 in sixty days." I knew that by my leading the people were confident to follow. My mind thought, *Buddy, you are in a real mess!* Yet my spirit was confident in God.

Six days later I was out of town for a meeting when my secretary called and said, "I couldn't wait until you returned to tell you: A letter came in the mail today and there was a check in it for $3,000 for you personally!"

"Glory to God! There is three fifths of my mission money!" The rest came on time.

God is going to perform and back His Word. That would not have worked had I not followed the pattern God gave us. I had to take the lead.

You rise or fall with your leadership. That is why some people have only grown so far and why some churches don't grow: Their leadership has not gone past a certain level, so they can't either.

A church can only go as far as its leadership.

> And the Lord spake unto Moses, saying, Send thou men, that they may search the land of Canaan...
>
> And Moses by the commandment of the Lord sent them from the wilderness of Paran: all those men were heads of the children of Israel.
>
> Numbers 13:1-3

Moses sent twelve men to spy out the Promised Land. These men were *heads* of the children of Israel. In other words, they were the leaders, the men in responsible positions of authority — a leadership that had been selected by God.

> And they went and came to Moses ... And they told him, and said, We came unto the land whither thou sentest us, and surely it floweth with milk and honey; and this is the fruit of it.
>
> Nevertheless the people be strong that dwell in the land, and the cities are walled, and very great...
>
> And Caleb, stilled the people before Moses, and said, Let us go up at once, and possess it; for we are well able to overcome it.
>
> But the men that went up with him said, We be not able to go up against the people; for they are stronger than we.

Leadership

And they brought up an evil report of the land which they had searched.
Numbers 13:26-32

There is a very important point about leadership in this passage of Scripture. Your leadership can get you to your Promised Land in a short time, or it can lead you in a circle for forty years. This is what happened to the children of Israel. Any person in decent physical condition could have walked to the Promised Land within six days; yet they wandered in the wilderness for forty years. They could not go beyond their leadership.

Where is your leadership leading you? What direction are they giving to your life? Are you getting there quickly, or is it taking an eternity? Are you in the wilderness?

As a result of the authority vested in the Israelite leaders, three and a half million people were led in a circle for forty years. That should impress upon you one thing: be careful who you are following.

Because all those men which have seen my glory, and my miracles, which I did in Egypt and in the wilderness, and have tempted me now these ten times, and have not hearkened to my voice;

Surely they shall not see the land which I sware unto their fathers, neither shall any of them that provoked me see it.

Numbers 14:22,23

The leadership you are under can keep you from walking in the fullness of what God has promised. Leadership is critical; we cannot treat it carelessly or haphazardly. Whenever I share God's Word, it is not only from the standpoint of a leader, but from your standpoint as a follower. The responsibility is upon the followers as well as the leaders. You are just as responsible because Jesus has made you free. You live in liberty!

Qualities of a Leader

When a man has the capabilities of leading you astray, then obviously he is going to hurt you. You need to examine whether leadership is good or bad. There must be qualities involved that will dictate what is correct and what is incorrect.

God has included guidelines in His Word that will help you to determine whether you are being led properly. Watch the man who is reaching for authority, he will hurt you; but help the

Leadership

man who is reaching for responsibility, he will bless you. The attitude of the person wanting power and authority will get him into trouble, while the attitude of the person wanting responsibility will only guide him in the right direction. Scripture to back this statement is found in Philippians 2:19-22:

But I trust in the Lord Jesus to send Timotheus shortly unto you, that I also may be of good comfort, when I know your state.

For I have no man likeminded, who will naturally care for your state.

For all seek their own, not the things which are Jesus Christ's.

These statements by Paul are vitally important. Timothy and Paul had presented themselves in service to the people as ministers of the Gospel. Timothy had the same goals in mind that Paul had: to serve the people, to bless them, to aid and assist them. Yet Paul didn't have anyone else who thought like Timothy. Timothy was after responsibility, not authority or power. The others had a different motive.

Motives are very important. A person can do the right thing for the wrong motive, and it will be wrong. Look at the motives behind your leadership.

A pastor's attitude should be to feed the flock. Again, I quote 1 Peter 5:2, which says:

Feed the flock of God which is among you, taking the oversight thereof, not by constraint, but willingly; not for filthy lucre, but of a ready mind.

This scripture is dealing with attitude because it says, **Feed the flock...not by constraint, but willingly....** What other way could it be done? **...for filthy lucre** (money).... If the motive of a pastor is money, he is in error. He should be **of a ready mind** and willing to do his job according to the Word of God.

The next verse says, **Neither as being lords over God's heritage, but being ensamples to the flock** (v. 3). Whose heritage is it? God's heritage. Many people who have taken their position in the Body of Christ as apostle, prophet, evangelist, pastor, or teacher try to dominate God's people. That is wrong.

Leadership

And when the chief Shepherd shall appear, ye shall receive a crown of glory that fadeth not away (v. 4). Jesus is the Chief Shepherd and we in the ministry are to act as undershepherds. However, this does not mean we are to rule, dominate, and deal harshly with the people. We must be sure to keep our motives right.

In the Third Epistle of John there is the illustration of a man who is reaching for authority and not responsibility. Verse 9 says, **I wrote unto the church: but Diotrephes, who loveth to have the preeminence among them, receiveth us not.** Notice the word **preeminence,** which means authority or rule. Diotrephes would not receive John. Where was his love?

In verse 10 John wrote, **Wherefore, if I come, I will remember his deeds which he doeth, prating against us with malicious words: and not content therewith, neither doth he himself receive the brethren, and forbiddeth them that would, and casteth them out of the church.** Any time you find a person who says, "We are a select group, and we only receive certain ones," look out! Everyone should be welcome. We are **born** into the Body of Christ, not **voted in!**

We must always remember that God loves the world—not just the believers, but the whole world! Does that mean God loves the homosexual, the drunkard, the prostitute, and the drug addict? Absolutely! Love does not condone what a person does, but it reaches out to them and freely offers the Word of God.

Do you think John would say, "Let's go ahead and love them, brethren. We'll just stay sweet"? If you think so, then look at verse 11: **Beloved, follow not that which is evil, but that which is good.** If your leadership is guiding you into evil, or any kind of wrongdoing, have the spiritual intelligence not to follow them. **Follow not that which is evil, but that which is good. He that doeth good is of God: but he that doeth evil hath not seen God.**

However, in verse 12 we find a man who is following after responsibility: **Demetrius hath good report of all men, and of the truth itself: yea, and we also**

Leadership

bear record; and ye know that our record is true. This man is given to truth, not preeminence of authority.

John is telling us very distinctly that we are not to follow after those who are going the wrong way, but to follow after those who are leading us correctly. We are to bless those who feed the flock and stay away from those who fleece the flock.

God said, **And I will give you pastors according to mine heart, which shall feed you with knowledge and understanding** (Jer. 3:15). The very heart of God is to feed the flock. Pastors sent by God will feed the flock with knowledge and understanding. If you are not receiving knowledge and understanding from your spiritual leadership, you are not being led properly.

And I will gather the remnant of my flock out of all countries whither I have driven them, and will bring them again to their folds; and they shall be fruitful and increase.

And I will set up shepherds over them which shall feed them: and they shall fear no more, nor be dismayed, neither shall they be lacking, saith the Lord.

Jeremiah 23:3,4

When you are fed the Word of God, certain results, or fruit, will be produced: There will be no more fear, dismay, or lack. This is how you are to judge your leadership. You are not to judge the leader, but you are to judge that which your leader is feeding you.

Ezekiel 34:23,24 is prophetically speaking of Jesus:

And I will set up one shepherd over them, and he shall feed them, even my servant David; he shall feed them, and he shall be their shepherd. And I the Lord will be their God, and my servant David a prince among them; I the Lord have spoken it.

Leadership is under a divine obligation to feed the flock. This 34th chapter of Ezekiel begins with these words:

And the word of the Lord came unto me, saying, Son of man, prophesy against the shepherds of Israel, prophesy, and say unto them, Thus saith the Lord God unto the shepherds; Woe be to the shepherds of Israel that do feed themselves! should not the shepherds feed the flocks?
Ye eat the fat, and ye clothe you with the wool, ye kill them that are fed: but ye feed not the flock (vv. 1-3).

When a shepherd is not feeding the flock, he is not pleasing to God. Your responsibility is not to try to keep that leader in line with God; the Word will do that.

Again, verse 3 says, **Ye eat the fat, and ye clothe you with the wool.** In other words, you either feed the flock because you love God, or you fleece the flock. The shepherds referred to here fleeced their flocks! Where do you think the wool came from? These shepherds took what belonged to their flocks.

A shepherd has an obligation to feed his flock, not take care of himself only. Spiritual law declares that when a shepherd feeds the flock, he will be taken care of; so don't go after money — God will supply your need. Operating in the law of action and reaction will produce the desired result.

They build up Zion with blood, and Jerusalem with iniquity.

The heads thereof judge for reward, and the priests thereof teach for hire, and the prophets thereof divine for money: yet will they lean upon the Lord, and say, Is not the Lord among us? none evil can come upon us.

Micah 3:10,11

These men, the leadership, have the wrong motive, the wrong purposes in mind. Ministers have fallen because they had wrong motives. They got power hungry or money hungry. More people have fallen because of those basic elements than any others.

But God has a better way. He does not intend for money to be our motive. When we lead people, money should not be our purpose. Our responsibility is to be a blessing to the Body of Christ.

Behold, the Lord God will come with strong hand, and his arm shall rule for him: behold, his reward is with him, and his work before him. He shall feed his flock like a shepherd: he shall gather the lambs with his arm, and carry them in his bosom, and shall gently lead those that are with young.

Isaiah 40:10,11

Those who are in positions of leadership and responsibility should operate gently. Much of the time people in responsible positions have a tendency to bark out a statement. As Teddy Roosevelt said, "Walk softly, but carry a big stick." In other words, you can be gentle, but still speak in a way that will cause everyone to recognize your authority. The area that must be dealt with is attitude.

Leadership

Some people think that a man can't be gentle. They labor under the misconception that a man must run his life like an army. I understand the element involved in discipline, but it is so much easier to follow the Bible pattern. Do it the Bible way: gently. One of the fruits of the Spirit which are mentioned in Galatians, chapter 5, is gentleness. If you want the fruit of the Spirit to be manifested in your life, some things need to be done gently.

Jesus operated in a gentle fashion. He took children in His arms, loved them and ministered to them. He was gentle, and He was a man. People sometimes look at His love side and take away from His manly side. If Jesus wasn't manly, how did He run the moneychangers out of the temple?

What about King David? He made this statement about the Lord in the Psalms: **...thy gentleness hath made me great** (Ps. 18:35). Here was a man who fought and defeated Goliath, a giant. King Saul had won his battles, but David had won tens of thousands. **...Saul hath**

slain his thousands, and David his ten thousands (1 Sam. 18:7). David had slain many, yet he was a gentle man.

Don't mistake gentleness for weakness; they are two entirely different things. Gentleness involves empathizing with people — not sympathizing, but gently helping them.

Woe be unto the pastors that destroy and scatter the sheep of my pasture! saith the Lord.

Therefore thus saith the Lord God of Israel against the pastors that feed my people; Ye have scattered my flock, and driven them away, and have not visited them: behold, I will visit upon you the evil of your doings, saith the Lord.

And I will gather the remnant of my flock out of all countries whither I have driven them, and will bring them again to their folds; and they shall be fruitful and increase.

Jeremiah 23:1-3

Bless those who **gather** the flock; watch those who **scatter** the flock. If the flock is scattering, something is wrong. Men who love God and are in responsible positions will gather the flock, not scatter them. There is a great difference between the man who says of the sheep, "They are God's," and the man who says, "They are mine." Psalm 100:3 says, **Know ye that the Lord he is God: it is he that hath made us, and not we ourselves; we are his people, and the sheep of his pasture.** In the New Testament we read, **…ye are not your own…ye are bought with a price** (1 Cor. 6:19,20).

The person who pays for something owns it, and God paid for his flock. We belong to God. The position of the pastor is as undershepherd. He is to feed, to care for, and to gently bless their lives. God has put pastors in the position of tenderly caring for His flock. If the pastor scatters the flock, it is wrong.

The Lord is my shepherd; I shall not want (Ps. 23:1). The Lord is the Shepherd. Referring again to the words of Ezekiel, we read:

And I will set up one shepherd over them, and he shall feed them, even my servant David; he shall feed them, and he shall be their shepherd.

And I the Lord will be their God, and my servant David a prince among them; I the Lord have spoken it.

Thus shall they know that I the Lord their God am with them, and that they, even the house of Israel, are my people, saith the Lord God.

And ye my flock, the flock of my pasture, are men, and I am your God, saith the Lord God.
Ezekiel 34:23,24,30,31

The sheep belong to God. No matter which pasture they are in, they are still a part of God's flock. For centuries men have debated that issue. The Apostle Paul wrote the Corinthian church:

Ye are yet carnal: for whereas there is among you envying, and strife, and divisions, are ye not carnal, and walk as men?

For while one saith, I am of Paul; and another, I am of Apollos; are ye not carnal?
1 Corinthians 3:3,4

While these arguments and debates went on in the Body of Christ, some did have enough sense to say, "I belong to Christ." We need to have that same intelligence today.

In Judges, chapter 8, after Gideon had won a battle, the people came to him. In verses 22 and 23 we read:

Then the men of Israel said unto Gideon, Rule thou over us, both thou, and thy son, and thy son's son also: for thou hast delivered us from the hand of Midian.

And Gideon said unto them, I will not rule over you, neither shall my son rule over you: the Lord shall rule over you.

Leadership

As God's child, you can know His voice.

You are to listen to the voice of your pastor only as long as he is teaching the Word of God. Paul said, **Be ye followers of me, even as I also am of Christ** (1 Cor. 11:1). Be very particular about who you follow and what you hear.

5
Submission or Obedience?

Again, I quote from Paul's letter to the church at Rome:

> Let every soul be subject unto the higher powers. For there is no power but of God: the powers that be are ordained of God.
>
> Whosoever therefore resisteth the power, resisteth the ordinance of God: and they that resist shall receive to themselves damnation.
>
> For rulers are not a terror to good works, but to the evil. Wilt thou then not be afraid of the power? do that which is good, and thou shalt have praise of the same.
>
> **Romans 13:1-3**

There is an important point made in verse 3. When something is good, it is God; when something is evil, it is not God. This becomes a key or clue in submission. God will not impose His will upon you; therefore, no man has that right. There are conditions to submission.

If it will produce good, then you are free to submit yourself in love.

Notice the phrase in verse 3, **For rulers are not a terror to good works, but to the evil.** The word *terror* is speaking of fear. Anything that produces terror, or fear, is not from God. **For God hath not given us the spirit of fear; but of power, and of love, and of a sound mind** (2 Tim. 1:7).

The Bible says that every good and perfect gift is from above. (James 1:17.) Most of the time we view this scripture in light of spiritual matters; but we should allow it to carry over into the natural realm, involving the things of this physical world. We should allow it to direct us in political areas. When a man is producing good, follow him. If his works produce evil — if they kill, steal, or destroy — he is not from God. Satan and evil are synonymous; God and good are synonymous.

Before you make decisions, ask yourself this question, "Is it producing good in my life, for my family and my nation?"

If submission calls you to death, then something is wrong. You may ask, "But

Submission or Obedience?

and who is that God that shall deliver you out of my hands?

Shadrach, Meshach, and Abednego, answered and said to the king, O Nebuchadnezzar, we are not careful to answer thee in this matter.

If it be so, our God whom we serve is able to deliver us from the burning fiery furnace, and he will deliver us out of thine hand, O king.

But if not, be it known unto thee, O king, that we will not serve thy gods, nor worship the golden image which thou hast set up.
Daniel 3:14-18

The king's order for everyone to worship his god was a violation of the principles of the Word of God. These three men had a choice to make. They could submit to this decree and be in total opposition to God's Word, or they could stand before the king, unwilling to bow. This was not rebellion by Shadrach, Meshach, and Abednego. They were willing to obey and serve Nebuchadnezzar as king, but they could not submit themselves in worship of his god. In making this choice, they realized that it could mean their lives; but they never considered any other alternative.

> Then was Nebuchadnezzar full of fury, and the form of his visage was changed against Shadrach, Meshach, and Abednego: therefore he spake, and commanded that they should heat the furnace one seven times more than it was wont to be heated.
>
> And he commanded the most mighty men that were in his army to bind Shadrach, Meshach, and Abednego, and to cast them into the burning fiery furnace...
>
> And these three men, Shadrach, Meshach, and Abednego, fell down bound into the midst of the burning fiery furnace.
>
> **Daniel 3:19-23**

Then Nebuchadnezzar looked into the furnace and said:

> ...Did not we cast three men bound into the midst of the fire? ...Lo, I see four men loose, walking in the midst of the fire, and they have no hurt; and the form of the fourth is like the Son of God.
>
> **Daniel 3:24,25**

These three Hebrew men chose to serve God rather than worship an idol, and Jesus delivered them! The fourth man that the king saw in the midst of the fire was Jesus!

When you are obedient to God and His Word, He will deliver you — no

Submission or Obedience?

matter what kind of situation you may be in or how drastic it may seem. God **will** deliver you!

And as they spake unto the people, the priests, and the captain of the temple, and the Sadducees, came upon them.

Being grieved that they taught the people, and preached through Jesus the resurrection of the dead.

And they laid hands on them, and put them in hold unto the next day: for it was now eventide.
Acts 4:1-3

These disciples were thrown in jail for preaching the Gospel. Then the next day they were brought before the high priest and elders.

And they called them, and commanded them not to speak at all nor teach in the name of Jesus.

But Peter and John answered and said unto them, Whether it be right in the sight of God to hearken unto you more than unto God, judge ye. For we cannot but speak the things which we have seen and heard.

So when they had further threatened them, they let them go, finding nothing how they might punish them, because of the people: for all men glorified God for that which was done.
Acts 4:18-21

The elders threatened these disciples and warned them never to speak again in the name of Jesus, but that didn't scare the disciples:

And being let go, they went to their own company, and reported all that the chief priests and elders had said unto them.

And when they heard that, they lifted up their voice to God with one accord...Lord, behold their threatenings: and grant unto thy servants, that with all boldness they may speak thy word.

By stretching forth thine hand to heal; and that signs and wonders may be done by the name of thy holy child Jesus.

Acts 4:23-30

They were kept in jail for only one day; then they returned to preaching the Gospel, even though it was against the orders of the high priest. The men in authority said they could do anything except use the name of Jesus. But there was a higher authority than those men. Jesus had already issued a higher order.

Go ye into all the world, and preach the gospel to every creature.

He that believeth and is baptized shall be saved; but he that believeth not shall be damned.

Submission or Obedience?

And these signs shall follow them that believe; In my name shall they cast out devils; they shall speak with new tongues;

They shall take up serpents; and if they drink any deadly thing, it shall not hurt them; they shall lay hands on the sick, and they shall recover.

Mark 16:15-18

And by the hands of the apostles were many signs and wonders wrought among the people...

Insomuch that they brought forth the sick into the streets, and laid them on beds and couches, that at the least the shadow of Peter passing by might overshadow some of them.

There came also a multitude out of the cities round about unto Jerusalem, bringing sick folks, and them which were vexed with unclean spirits: and they were healed every one.

Then the high priest rose up, and all they that were with him, (which is the sect of the Sadducees,) and were filled with indignation, And laid their hands on the apostles, and put them in the common prison.

But the angel of the Lord by night opened the prison doors, and brought them forth, and said,

Go, stand and speak in the temple to the people all the words of this life.

Acts 5:12-20

The angel of God is a representative of God. The words an angel speaks carry the same authority as God's Word. It was God's messenger who instructed the apostles to preach the Gospel, regardless of what the high priest had told them; and that higher authority prevailed. The angel told the apostles to go to the temple and preach, so the next morning they entered the temple and taught.

...But the high priest came, and they that were with him, and called the council together, and all the senate of the children of Israel, and sent to the prison to have them brought.

But when the officers came, and found them not in prison, they returned, and told, saying, The prison truly found we shut with all safety, and the keepers standing without before the doors: but when we had opened, we found no man within...

Then came one and told them, saying, Behold, the men whom ye put in prison are standing in the temple, and teaching the people.

Then went the captain with the officers, and brought them...And when they had brought them, they set them before the council: and the high priest asked them, saying, Did not we straitly command you that ye should not teach in this name? and, behold, ye have filled

Submission or Obedience?

Jerusalem with your doctrine, and intend to bring this man's blood upon us.

Then Peter and the other apostles answered and said, We ought to obey God rather than men.
Acts 5:21-29

It is a Bible principle that we are to obey God as the supreme authority. Then we are to obey and submit to man as long as he is following God.

The Book of Joshua, chapter 2, describes how a harlot named Rahab was honored for giving aid to the Israelite spies. Rahab chose to believe God's Word, even though it was in violation of the laws of the land. She chose to submit to the higher authority. She hid the spies from the king's men, then hung a scarlet rope over the wall, allowing the Israelites to escape. The fact that it was a scarlet rope is significant because red represents the blood of Christ, and we have been redeemed by His blood. Through it, we obtain escape, deliverance, and protection.

And the Lord said unto Samuel, How long wilt thou mourn for Saul, seeing I have rejected him from reigning over Israel? fill thine horn with

oil, and go, I will send thee to Jesse the Bethlehemite: for I have provided me a king among his sons.

And Samuel said, How can I go? if Saul hear it, he will kill me.
1 Samuel 16:1,2

As far as God is concerned, Saul is no longer the king over Israel; so God tells Samuel to go and anoint a shepherd boy named David as king. But Saul is still king! Can you imagine the dilemma that Samuel was in? He has been given a command by God, but his fleshly man is not wanting to obey. If he anoints David and Saul finds out about it, Samuel could be killed.

Which authority must Samuel consider as supreme? There is no choice. God is the higher authority, and Samuel knows that. He must be willing to act as God has instructed him and go in faith, regardless of how the circumstances may look. But God makes a way by which Samuel can be obedient to Him and not lose his life: **And the Lord said, Take an heifer with thee, and say, I am come to sacrifice to the Lord** (v. 2).

Submission or Obedience?

In 1 Samuel, chapter 19, we find Saul's son Jonathan in the same kind of dilemma: **And Saul spake to Jonathan his son, and to all his servants, that they should kill David** (v. 1).

There is a double problem here: not only is Jonathan Saul's son, he is also David's best friend. He has been commanded by his father to kill his best friend. What is he to do? Some would reason that, regardless of what he was told to do, Jonathan ought to obey his father.

The only way to make a decision is to establish who has the higher authority. Will the end result be good or evil? Jonathan has a command from his father, but the law of God says he is not to take another man's life. Which law has the supreme authority? The answer is very simple: that which produces good.

In order for it to operate correctly, authority must be held in the proper sense. We are to exercise authority over our children, but not harm them.

If you follow after a leader who is producing evil or wrong, stop following him. God does not expect you to submit your life to people just so they can kill you. Even though they may have authority in this life, there is a higher authority involved. We can see this in the example of Paul (then known as Saul) in the New Testament.

And after that many days were fulfilled, the Jews took counsel to kill him:

But their laying await was known of Saul. And they watched the gates day and night to kill him.

Then the disciples took him by night, and let him down by the wall in a basket.
Acts 9:23-25

The following passage contains another example of obeying the higher of the two authorities. Paul and Barnabas obeyed God rather than the Jewish leaders.

And it came to pass in Iconium, that they (Paul and Barnabas) went both together into the synagogue of the Jews, and so spake, that a great multitude both of the Jews and also of the Greeks believed.

But the unbelieving Jews stirred up the Gentiles, and made their minds evil affected against the brethren.

Submission or Obedience?

aren't you supposed to be willing to lay down your life for God?" Remember, the Word of God teaches that we are to lay down the old life and present the new life to God. But if it is a matter of laying down your life to be taken, it is not God. We are to live life to its fullest. God wants us to reign supreme on the earth — and that does not include getting ourselves killed.

Submission and obedience are not the same. Obedience is an action; submission is an attitude of the heart.

The Word of God says we are to submit ourselves to one another in love. (Eph. 5:21.) This does not mean we are to obey everything we are told. We are not to submit to some people simply because they are our elders. There is a higher power and authority that we are to follow. Submission is not unquestioned obedience to authority. You need to ask questions. There will be times that you have a check in your spirit, which will be your conscience. You need to recognize the level of authority that is supreme. If you violate your heart, you will be violating the principles of God.

Submission is not a blind response to any order.

Submission is a willingness to follow leadership as long as it does not violate God's Word. You are to follow your leaders as long as they follow God. Should they ever get off track, you are expected to keep following God.

There are illustrations from the Word of God that will emphasize this truth. In Daniel, chapter 3, King Nebuchadnezzar had set forth a decree that said all people were to worship a golden image which he had made. His instructions to the people were that when they heard the sound of musical instruments and singing, they were to bow down and worship the golden image. However, three young Hebrew men, who refused to worship this pagan god, were brought before the king.

Nebuchadnezzar spake and said unto them, Is it true, O Shadrach, Meshach, and Abednego, do not ye serve my gods, nor worship the golden image which I have set up?

...if ye worship not, ye shall be cast the same hour into the midst of a burning fiery furnace;

Submission or Obedience?

Long time therefore abode they speaking boldly in the Lord, which gave testimony unto the word of his grace, and granted signs and wonders to be done by their hands.

But the multitude of the city was divided: and part held with the Jews, and part with the apostles.

And when there was an assault made both of the Gentiles, and also of the Jews with their rulers, to use them despitefully, and to stone them,

They were ware of it, and fled unto Lystra and Derbe, cities of Lycaonia, and unto the region that lieth round about:

And there they preached the gospel.
                                        Acts 14:1-7

These Jewish leaders were producing wrong. The key is to be led to good.

But the Jews which believed not, moved with envy, took unto them certain lewd fellows of the baser sort, and gathered a company, and set all the city on an uproar, and assaulted the house of Jason, and sought to bring them out to the people.

And when they found them not, they drew Jason and certain brethren unto the rulers of the city, crying, These that have turned the world upside down are come hither also.

Whom Jason hath received: and these all do contrary to the decrees of Caesar, saying that there is another king, one Jesus.

Acts 17:5-7

Again we see the issue: Who has the higher authority: Caesar or Jesus?

Without knowledge of the higher authority, the natural human mind will say that we are to worship the king. We do have an allegiance to the President of the United States and to our nation. America is the greatest land that has ever been, and we are to serve it fully and wholeheartedly. But if it comes to making a decision between your country and God, there is no question about which you are to follow.

We have read about men who have faced confrontations and decisions in regard to authority. Now I want to point to some women who faced the same type of situation.

And the Egyptians made the children of Israel to serve with rigour.
And they made their lives bitter with hard bondage, in morter, and in brick, and in all manner of service in the field: all their service, wherein they made them serve, was with rigour.

Exodus 1:13,14

Leadership

The Egyptians had total control over Israel at this time, and they worked them just as hard as they could. They ruled and reigned over the children of Israel without mercy.

There is nothing wrong with submitting yourself to someone to work for him when it is done in love. However, leaders are not to be hard and merciless. God does not have a leader in mind that will rule with force, threat, or terror.

And the king of Egypt spake to the Hebrew midwives, of which the name of the one was Shiphrah, and the name of the other Puah:

And he said, When ye do the office of a midwife to the Hebrew women, and see them upon the stools; if it be a son, then ye shall kill him: but if it be a daughter, then she shall live.

But the midwives feared God, and did not as the king of Egypt commanded them, but saved the men children alive.

Exodus 1:15-17

These Hebrew midwives were not in rebellion, but were acknowledging the law of the higher authority. We must always obey the Word of God above **any** order we receive.

And the midwives said unto Pharaoh, Because the Hebrew women are not as the Egyptian women; for they are lively, and are delivered ere the midwives come in unto them.

Therefore God dealt well with the midwives: and the people multiplied, and waxed very mighty.

And it came to pass, because the midwives feared God, that he made them houses.
Exodus 1:19-21

It pays to be obedient to God. Even though it may look as if it will cost you, you will always get results when you follow after the higher authority.

6
Ruling With Liberty

Stand fast therefore in the liberty wherewith Christ hath made us free, and be not entangled again with the yoke of bondage.

Galatians 5:1

There are people who have been born of the Spirit of God, receiving the liberty of Jesus, but then returned unto bondage. When people say you must do certain things in order to conform, don't believe it unless you find it in God's Word. The people in the Galatian church were being told that they had to be circumcised to be saved, so the Apostle Paul wrote them and boldly stated, **Be not entangled again with the yoke of bondage.**

As a Christian, you have been made free in Jesus Christ. Don't go back into bondage through the Law. In John 8:36 Jesus said, **If the Son therefore shall make you free, ye shall be free indeed.** That settles it! Jesus has made you free.

To put yourself back under the Law is to commit spiritual adultery — to take yourself from beneath the marriage relationship that you had with Christ and put yourself under that old relationship.

It seems to be a very easy thing for people to return to bondage. The principle of slavery has always existed, both in spirit and in body. It is easier to be a slave than to be a leader.

In verse 13 of Galatians 5 Paul addresses the other side of this issue:

For, brethren, ye have been called unto liberty; only use not liberty for an occasion to the flesh, but by love serve one another.

Don't allow your liberty to cause you to operate in the flesh. When some people find out they are free, they think they are free to float with the breeze, just going wherever they want, when they want. They jump from one extreme to the other, from total bondage to total "freedom."

Let's look at a parable in the ninth chapter of Judges:

The trees went forth on a time to anoint a king over them; and they said unto the olive tree, Reign thou over us.

But the olive tree said unto them, Should I leave my fatness, wherewith by me they honour God and man, and go to be promoted over the trees?
Judges 9:8,9

The olive tree bears olives, and olives produce an oil which is a type of anointing. When the trees say, "Come, rule and reign over us," the olive tree answers, "Should I give up my anointing? Should I quit producing where I am in order to rule over you?"

It is a divine law of God which says that when you don't bear fruit, you will be cut off. In the natural world, if you don't produce on the job, you will get fired.

And the trees said to the fig tree, Come thou, and reign over us.

But the fig tree said unto them, Should I forsake my sweetness, and my good fruit, and go to be promoted over the trees?
Judges 9:10,11

The fig represents the sweetness of life. Should the fig tree quit producing in order to rule and reign? The answer is no. You have to operate and function in the anointing that is upon you.

Then said the trees unto the vine, Come thou, and reign over us.

And the vine said unto them, Should I leave my wine, which cheereth God and man, and go to be promoted over the trees?

Judges 9:12,13

The vine produces joy, cheer. Should it stop producing joy in order to rule? No.

Then said all the trees unto the bramble, Come thou, and reign over us.

And the bramble said unto the trees, If in truth ye anoint me king over you, then come and put your trust in my shadow: and if not, let fire come out of the bramble, and devour the cedars of Lebanon.

Judges 9:14,15

What does a bramble produce? Thorns and thistles. When you are always looking for someone to rule over you, you will eventually end up with the wrong person. Notice the bramble said, **Come and put your trust in my shadow.** That ought to tell you something, because there are no shadows with God. **God is light, and in him is no darkness at all** (1 John 1:5).

In John 15 Jesus says to His disciples:

Ruling With Liberty

I am the true vine, and my Father is the husbandman.

Every branch in me that beareth not fruit he taketh away: and every branch that beareth fruit, he purgeth it, that it may bring forth more fruit.

...As the branch cannot bear fruit of itself, except it abide in the vine; no more can ye, except ye abide in me.

I am the vine, ye are the branches: He that abideth in me, and I in him, the same bringeth forth much fruit: for without me ye can do nothing.

John 15:1-5

There is a progression in these verses. First, the branch bears fruit. Then a purging comes which brings forth **more fruit.** Finally, Jesus speaks of the importance of abiding in Him, which will bring forth **much fruit.** It is not enough just to bear fruit.

This is the word that came unto Jeremiah from the Lord, after that the king Zedekiah had made a covenant with all the people which were at Jerusalem, to proclaim liberty unto them;

That every man should let his manservant, and every man his maidservant, being an Hebrew or an Hebrewess, go free; that none should serve himself of them to wit, of a Jew his brother.

Jeremiah 34:8,9

You must understand that God is still working today according to these same principles. His methods may have changed, but His principles remain the same. God wants liberty; He wants people set free. He makes no distinction regarding how they got into bondage. All He cares about is seeing them set free.

The only bondage we should have is to love. We are to submit to one another in love. Love should be the controlling and motivating factor in all that we do.

The love of God is likened to the mortar that holds bricks together. That love will cause a bond and a strength in the place you are functioning.

Again, I quote from Jeremiah, chapter 34:

But afterward they turned, and caused the servants and the handmaids, whom they had let go free, to return, and brought them into subjection for servants and for handmaids.

Therefore the word of the Lord came to Jeremiah from the Lord, saying,

Thus saith the Lord, the God of Israel; I made a covenant with your fathers in the day that I brought them forth out of the land of Egypt, out of the house of bondmen, saying,

At the end of seven years let ye go every man his brother an Hebrew, which hath been sold unto thee; and when he hath served thee six years, thou shalt let him go free from thee: but your fathers hearkened not unto me, neither inclined their ear.

And ye were now turned, and had done right in my sight, in proclaiming liberty every man to his neighbour; and ye had made a covenant before me in the house which is called by my name:

But ye turned and polluted my name, and caused every man his servant, and every man his handmaid, whom he had set at liberty at their pleasure, to return, and brought them into subjection, to be unto you for servants and for handmaids.

Jeremiah 34:11-16

The dangerous part occurs when a person or group puts someone back into bondage without authority to do so.

Therefore thus saith the Lord: Ye have not hearkened unto me, in proclaiming liberty, every one to his brother, and every man to his neighbour: behold, I proclaim a liberty for you, saith the Lord, to the sword, to the pestilence, and to the famine; and I will make you to be removed into all the kingdoms of the earth.

Jeremiah 34:17

If any person tries to exercise authority over you and put you into bondage, that person will be pulled down and his position brought to naught. He will destroy himself if he fails to do what the Spirit of the Lord tells him.

When we don't walk in liberty, the glory of the Lord will depart. Living in this nation proves that. We fight for liberty.

A Challenge...

As I mentioned earlier in this book, authority comes three ways: by birth, by training, and by impartation. Ministers have said to me that they would love to be where I am in the Kingdom of God, that they esteem me and my position. (This is their attitude, not necessarily mine.)

Men have said to me, "How did you get where you are and how do you carry the authority that you have?" I want to tell the secret now:

First, I started with the authority that I received by birth, which was the ability to hear music. I couldn't read it, but I could sing the different parts with time and rhythm, leading others in it. Using that authority, I became a choir director in my home church.

Then I took a full-time position in Minneapolis, Minnesota, as music youth director. Even when I couldn't read music, I had musical ability that was placed in me at birth by God. My granddad could sing, my daddy could sing, and I could sing.

By study and training I cultivated my ability further. That authority carried me from there to a position with Brother Hagin. I worked as platform man in his meetings and office manager at home. The second thrust of authority came by training to run Brother Hagin's office. For a period of time I read one book each day on management. I learned how to manage people, time, and money.

As I disciplined myself, the level of authority intensified and was recognized. As I was faithful in the authority given by birth, and diligent in the authority obtained through training, there came a third thrust of authority. This level came by impartation. In November, 1977, God called me to pastor. At that moment it was as though He cut me open and dropped down inside me the ability to pastor. By His Spirit, God imparted to me authority to lead His people.

In November, 1981, I entered into another realm of authority, not by my intention or design, but by God's. He has told me to serve as pastor to pastors and ministers. I am a leader of leaders.

Many of you can do the same this day. I challenge you to arise and start with the authority that you were given by birth. By discipline and training, you will receive more authority. By being faithful and obedient, God will impart even more, and you will fulfill the leadership position that God has called you to.

I challenge you to move out. There is work to be done for the Kingdom.

Then the men of Israel said unto Gideon, Rule thou over us, both thou, and thy son, and thy son's son also: for thou hast delivered us from the hand of Midian.
And Gideon said unto them, I will not rule over you, neither shall my son rule over you: the Lord shall rule over you.

Judges 8:22,23

Buddy Harrison is a man of love with a vision for the supernatural Church. He and his wife Pat move in the gifts of the Spirit with sensitivity and understanding.

As a small boy, Buddy was healed of paralyzing polio. Over 20 years ago he answered the call of God on his life and entered the ministry in the office of helps and as a singer of psalms and spiritual songs. He served Kenneth Hagin Ministries for ten years as office manager and pioneered many areas as an administrator.

In 1977 the Spirit of the Lord instructed Buddy to start Faith Christian Fellowship — a family church, teaching center, and world outreach in Tulsa, Oklahoma. There are now over 160 Faith Christian Fellowship affiliate churches spanning the U.S., Canada, Jamaica, and Europe; 15 U.S. Bible schools; 10 international Bible schools; and over 1,000 ordained and licensed ministers with FCF.

Buddy is an excellent teacher of the Word of God with the ability to communicate the principles from the Word with a New Testament love. He attributes any success he has to being obedient to the Spirit of God and living the Word, whatever the cost.

He is currently Founder/President of Faith Christian Fellowship and Founder/President of Harrison House.

Buddy and Pat have raised their two daughters, Cookie and Candy, and now reside in Tulsa with their son Damon.

To contact Dr. Harrison,
write:

Dr. Doyle Harrison
P. O. Box 35443
Tulsa, OK 74153

BOOKS BY BUDDY HARRISON

*Understanding Authority
For Effective Leadership*

Count It All Joy
Eight Principles To Use For Victory In Times Of
Temptations, Tests, & Trials

Coauthored by Van Gale

MERCY — The Gift Before and Beyond Faith

Coauthored by Michael Landsman

Maintaining a Spirit Filled Life

Available from your local bookstore.

HARRISON HOUSE
P. O. Box 35035 • Tulsa, OK 74153